THE HEYDAY
OF STEAM AROUND MANCHESTER

TOM HEAVYSIDE

IAN ALLAN
Publishing

First published 1995

ISBN 0 7110 2329 8

© Ian Allan Ltd 1995

Designed by Alan C. Butcher

Published by Ian Allan Publishing

an imprint of Ian Allan Ltd, Terminal House, Station Approach, Shepperton, Surrey TW17 8AS.
Printed by Ian Allan Printing Ltd, Coombelands House, Coombelands Lane, Addlestone, Weybridge, Surrey KT15 1HY.

Front Cover:
Manchester London Road. Making a sure-footed departure with 'The Mancunian', the 9.35am to London Euston, arguably Manchester's most prestigious train, which ran non-stop to the capital, is Longsight-based rebuilt three-cylinder 'Royal Scot' class 4-6-0 No 46106 *Gordon Highlander* — the only member of the class fitted with straight-sided smoke deflectors, which gave it a unique appearance — on 2 March 1960. At the time extensive work was in progress in preparation for the introduction of electric traction using the 25kV overhead system, which commenced between Manchester and Crewe on 12 September 1960 and resulted in the elimination of much steam working. The station was then renamed Manchester Piccadilly. *R. E. Gee*

Previous page:
The LNWR opened the Stalybridge-Diggle Junction via Micklehurst route on 1 December 1885, effectively as a relief line to that which it had constructed on the western side of the valley through Greenfield in 1849. Four stations were provided but they had all been closed by January 1917 and, while the occasional passenger train used the rails until September 1964, its main *raison d'être* was freight traffic. This ceased from 31 October 1966.

A few days before closure one-time Western Region BR Standard 'Britannia' Pacific No 70015 *Apollo* — then based at Stockport (Edgeley) — makes a fine sight near Friezland, heading up-grade into the Pennines, with an eastbound freight on 25 October 1966. Notice the name has been painted on the smoke deflector in place of the original cast plate. The late summer of 1967 saw the demise of this locomotive from Carlisle (Kingmoor) (12A) shed. *Don Cash*

Introduction

Manchester came to have a significant place in railway history with the opening of the George Stephenson-engineered Liverpool & Manchester Railway in 1830, an event often looked upon as the progenitor of the national system. However, on the outskirts of the region covered by this volume, the Bolton & Leigh Railway led the way, having commenced business two years earlier in 1828.

The subsequent development of the railway network in this important northern conurbation is a far too detailed and complex story to relate here. Sufficient to say that, by the end of the Victorian era, lines seemingly radiated out from the centre in all directions which, together with those that criss-crossed the area, formed a veritable web of inter-laced track-work.

At the turn of the century a multiplicity of companies had substantial interests in the region — some competing fiercely with each other for the traffic on offer, both passenger and goods. As a guide to the importance attached to Manchester by the railway barons one needs look no further than the one-time choice of routes available to London — to Euston by the London & North Western Railway, St Pancras via the Midland, Marylebone by courtesy of the Great Central or King's Cross over Great Northern metals — all featured in the timetables of yesteryear.

At the 1923 Grouping, the Great Central and Great Northern interests were absorbed by the London & North Eastern Railway, while the assets of the other companies were brought under the umbrella of the London Midland & Scottish Railway. Thus, on Nationalisation in 1948, the Eastern, as well as the London Midland Region of British Railways, came to have a strong foothold in the area.

During the early years of BR traffic throughout the region covered by this volume, roughly 20 miles from the city centre, was intense by any standards. While main line expresses whisked travellers afar, a frequent service of semi-fast and stopping trains along many routes catered for the daily needs of the local population. In addition, thousands of tons of freight of every description had to be transported in and out of the city, and the surrounding towns, each week.

The enormity and diversity of the stock of motive power maintained in the region in BR times can best be appreciated by a few statistics. For instance in September 1950, prior to the advent of the BR Standard classes, there were 913 steam locomotives, of almost every power classification from 0F to 7P, domiciled at 14 depots. These sheds are those that could normally be visited in and around Manchester on a day's itinerary following the route advised by that indispensable reference book *The British Locomotive Shed Directory*, together with the two in Stockport (Edgeley and Heaton Mersey), Macclesfield, Lees (Oldham), Bury and the two in Bolton — Bolton itself and Plodder Lane.

The total comprised 242 ex-LNER engines of 19 different classes dispersed between Gorton (the one Manchester shed under Eastern Region control), Heaton Mersey and Trafford Park, except for a solitary Thompson 'B1' class 4-6-0 No 61326 based at Newton Heath. Former LMS types totalled 661 of no less than 31 classes, including 95 elderly ex-Lancashire & Yorkshire Railway engines of five different designs. The balance was made up by 10 ex-WD '8F' 2-8-0s.

In addition, many other sheds, ranging from Kentish Town and Camden in the south to Polmadie in Glasgow, had regular duties to Manchester. Some of these diagrams utilised types

Left:
A view from the footplate of BR Standard Class 5 4-6-0 No 73142 approaching Salford (Irwell Street Goods Yard is just to the right of the engine) with a Llandudno-Manchester Exchange train on 14 May 1966. Thirty of the class were fitted with Caprotti valve gear, rather than the more conventional Walschaerts, and by 1964 all 20 of the English-based examples were on the books of Patricroft shed. No 73142 was withdrawn from there in May 1968 after a life of only 12 years; even so it had managed to outlive most of the class. *David C. Rodgers*

not normally shedded in the area, perhaps the most notable being the use of Gresley 'A3' Pacifics on Marylebone trains out of Manchester London Road, including on occasions the renowned No 60103 *Flying Scotsman*. From the foregoing it will readily be realised that Manchester and its environs offered a rich variety of steam power for the observer to savour.

Not unnaturally some routes were early targets for the elimination of steam, a process in fact begun as far back as 1913 when the L&YR experimentally electrified the Holcombe Brook branch from Bury using overhead wires. However, the railway then decided on a 1,200V dc side-contact system for the Manchester Victoria-Bury Bolton Street line which was energised in 1916, the Holcombe route being similarly modified in 1918. Then, in 1931, the Manchester South Junction & Altrincham line, jointly owned by the LMS and LNER, was converted for use by electric units collecting current at 1,500V dc from overhead wires.

The first significant dent in the steam empire during BR days was felt in 1954 by the electrification at 1,500V dc of the difficult Manchester-Sheffield via Woodhead line, along with some related branches. By the end of the decade a new threat to steam's long-term survival was much in evidence, with diesel locomotives making their presence felt and many local services being operated by diesel multiple-units.

However, in March 1959 the area's steam stud was still 736 strong, the LNER stable having been reduced to 98 of 12 different types, while the LMS stock numbered 532 (including 43 ex-L&YR engines) of 27 classes. Comparative newcomers were 43 BR Standard locomotives of six designs, while the strength of the ex-WD 2-8-0s had increased to 63. The locomotives were resident at 12 sheds; Belle Vue and Plodder Lane had become early casualties in the run down of steam.

The next body blow to the health of the steam locomotive was dealt in September 1960 with the inauguration, between Manchester and Crewe, of the first stage of the West Coast main line 25kV electrification scheme. Nevertheless, despite the ever-increasing diesel and electric onslaught and some rationalisation of services, in April 1965 359 steam locomotives remained in the area. These were allocated to eight sheds. While no former LNER or ex-WD engines remained, and all the pre-Grouping-built engines had been condemned, some 11 ex-LMS classes were represented among the 298 built to their designs. These were augmented by 61 BR Standard locomotives of five classes.

Fortuitously, Manchester remained one of the last bastions of steam almost until the bitter end, with six sheds surviving into 1968 and the last three not bolting their doors to the iron horse until 1 July — just six weeks before the fateful 15 guinea special ran on 11 August. Rightfully this passed through Manchester on its melancholy, if somewhat defiant, journey from Liverpool to Carlisle and back.

As a native of Westhoughton, on the fringe of the region depicted, and living there throughout the 1950s and 1960s in sight of Horwich Locomotive Works, albeit two miles away across open fields, the compilation of this album has been a fascinating step back in time. It can perforce only provide a snapshot of the voluminous number of steam passenger and freight turns which abounded during this era, but I trust some at least of the very varied atmosphere that prevailed has been conveyed. For many people this period was the heyday of steam.

It would be remiss of me not to place on record my indebtedness to the many photographers who, in response to my requests, kindly forwarded their precious gems for consideration in this volume, indeed some welcomed me to their homes for what became feasts of pure unadulterated nostalgia. My sincere thanks go to all who have contributed by way of slides or otherwise to making this memorial to Manchester area BR steam possible.

Tom Heavyside
Bolton
September 1994

Right:
The former Great Central side of Manchester London Road had platforms numbered A, B and C and once operated as a quite distinct entity from the ex-LNWR side. By 1954 overhead wires energised at 1,500V dc were in place at these platforms in connection with the Woodhead electrification scheme. Here the driver of Gorton-based Class A5 4-6-2T No 69822 enjoys the sunshine, while reversing into the station, on 20 July 1958. The 'A5s' were designed by Robinson and first built in 1911. No 69822 was withdrawn by November 1958. *R. E. Gee*

Right:
The Ian Allan *Trains Illustrated-*sponsored 'Pennine Limited' excursion approaches Stockport Edgeley, over the 600yd-long Mersey Viaduct, on its Leeds City-Crewe leg behind three-cylinder Compound 4-4-0s Nos 41100 and 41063 on 26 April 1958. The train had started at King's Cross and returned to London Euston. The Compounds were a familiar sight around Manchester, with Agecroft, Bolton, Longsight and Trafford Park all having an allocation in 1950. *Norman Harrop*

5

Above:
With an express passenger train emanating from Manchester London Road on 15 June 1957 'Patriot' class 4-6-0 No 45519 *Lady Godiva* gets into its stride passing Longsight station — the suffix Belle Vue related to the nearby pleasure gardens which attracted many special excursions. The station closed on 15 September 1958. The gardens have also closed. At the time *Lady Godiva* was allocated to Longsight shed, which is out of the picture on the right. Note, too, the splendid LNWR signal gantry. *W. Oliver/Colour-Rail*

Right:
LMS '3F' 0-6-0T 'Jinty' No 47528 shunts the carriage sidings at Longsight in 1957. Longsight shed (9A) can be seen in the background, No 47528 being based there throughout the 1950s and until its withdrawal in March 1960.

Longsight shed dates from 1842, the Manchester & Birmingham Railway also siting its locomotive works here. Later it was to become part of the LNWR empire. Ultimately, there were two sheds — north and south — with 12 roads in each, four linking the two buildings. In 1950 the Longsight shed foreman had charge of 129 former LMS-owned engines of 17 different species, the most powerful passenger types, all 4-6-0s, being 13 'Royal Scots', 15 'Jubilees' and seven 'Patriots'. Other well represented classes were 19 'Crab' 2-6-0s and 17 'Black 5' 4-6-0s along with a similar number of LMS 2-6-4Ts. In 1959 the named 4-6-0s accounted for 28 of the 105 locomotives on the books, which then included four 'Britannia' Pacifics. The shed closed to steam on 14 February 1965 in order to concentrate on the maintenance of diesel and electric traction. Today the depot continues to provide a similar service. *W. Oliver/Colour-Rail*

Left:
Some hazy sunshine on a frosty 18 January 1964 highlights Swindon-built BR Standard Class 4 4-6-0 No 75034 approaching Stockport No 2 signalbox, at the north end of Stockport Edgeley station, with a short parcels train from Manchester. At the time No 75034 was a Stoke & Cockshute (5D) engine, being sent for scrap during the autumn of 1966. *Brian Magilton*

Left:
'Britannia' Pacific No 70013 *Oliver Cromwell* achieved celebrity status when it became the last steam locomotive overhauled by BR, leaving Crewe Works on 2 February 1967. Later, at the end of 1967, when the rest of the surviving members of the class were retired, No 70013 was transferred to Carnforth (10A), to be retained specifically for use on specials during the dying months of steam and was, therefore, kept in exemplary condition.

On 13 April 1968 BR Scottish Region ran an Edinburgh-Stafford excursion with *Oliver Cromwell* at the head from Hellifield to Stockport via Blackburn and back to Carnforth via Wigan, seen here leaving Stockport Edgeley on the return journey. No 70013 also shared in working the last BR steam train on 11 August 1968 hauling the Manchester Victoria-Carlisle via Blackburn leg, before returning to its original stamping ground in East Anglia for preservation at Bressingham Steam Museum, near Diss, Norfolk.

The scene is reminiscent of the 1950s (apart from the catenary) when Longsight shed utilised its allocation of 'Britannias' — Nos 70031-33 and 70043/44 — on Manchester-London diagrams. Stockport was usually the last call on the return journey north before arrival in Manchester. *Neville Fields*

The Ivatt-designed LMS taper-boiler Class 2 2-6-2Ts, first built in 1946, were identical to the Class 2 2-6-0s, Nos 46400-527, introduced at the same time, except for the provision of side-tanks and coal bunker in place of a tender. The class incorporated many labour-saving features, such as self-cleaning smokeboxes, rocking grates and self-emptying ashpans.

No 41202 was transferred to Stockport (Edgeley) shed in August 1965, one of a quartet from Llandudno Junction (6G), and on 14 May 1966 was employed as Stockport station pilot. It is seen here having just attached some carriages to a southbound train. The engines were ideal for this type of work, the cut-away bunker sides allowing the crew good vision when working in reverse gear. On the right a BR Standard Class 9F 2-10-0 approaches light engine, whilst a local DMU service arrives from Manchester Piccadilly.
Alan C. Gilbert

Left:
Opened in 1883 by the LNWR the eight-road Stockport (Edgeley) shed was given the code 9B by the LMS in 1935, this being retained until the end of its days in May 1968. Historically the shed never had the more glamorous named express locomotives at its disposal, these normally being maintained down the road at its parent depot Longsight. But matters changed in the summer of 1962 with the unprecedented relocation of three 'Jubilee' 4-6-0s to Stockport. Then, even more noteworthy, in May 1965 the shed welcomed three 'Britannia' class Pacifics, including former 'Golden Arrow' engine No 70004 *William Shakespeare*, to be joined later by two more.

During the 1960s the total number of engines at 9B increased from 26 at the start of the decade to 39 on 1 January 1967, four of the 'Britannias' remaining at this date along with 17 'Black 5' 4-6-0s and 18 Stanier '8F' 2-8-0s. Resting inside the shed on 17 September 1966 is Ivatt Class 2 2-6-2T No 41233, which arrived on the Stockport scene in August 1965, seen alongside 'Britannia' No 70015 *Apollo*. No 41233 was withdrawn two months later.
Brian Magilton

Right:
Fowler-designed LMS parallel-boiler Class 4 2-6-4T No 42398 is photographed on the centre road at Macclesfield Central before working back to Manchester on 16 July 1957. While No 42398 was a Longsight engine, drivers at Macclesfield shed (9C) — by Macclesfield (Hibel Road) station — were well versed in handling these locomotives for virtually the class had exclusive rights to the shed during the 1950s. Eleven of the type had sole occupancy in 1950. Six remained in 1959, including one with the refinement of a side-window cab and doors similar to No 42398. Macclesfield shed ceased operation on 12 June 1961. *W. Oliver/Colour-Rail*

Above:
An unidentified inside-cylindered
LNWR Class 7F 0-8-0 potters along
near Handforth with a short
engineers' train in 1959. Much of
the infrastructure is already in place
for the forthcoming electrification of
the route from Manchester to Crewe
and beyond. These engines were
some of the few not to carry
smokebox numberplates, a veritable
nuisance to easy identification,
although it is highly likely that the
engine is one of the quartet on the
books at Stockport (Edgeley) in
1959. In the early part of the year
Longsight also had a couple of these
rather ungainly machines.
Norman Harrop

Left:
Trafford Park (9E) Fairburn Class 4 2-6-4T No 42079 catches the sunlight outside the magnificent 210ft single-span trainshed at Manchester Central on 4 March 1967. The span of this building was second only in width to the 240ft single span roof at London St Pancras. The locomotive was waiting to leave with the joint Stephenson Locomotive Society/Manchester Locomotive Society 'High Peak' railtour. This ex-Cheshire Lines Committee station opened in 1880, replacing a nearby temporary terminus of 1877, but the continuing BR rationalisation programme throughout the 1960s meant that its future became in doubt and closure took place on 5 May 1969. With the trainshed enjoying listed building status demolition was not an option and, after a period of almost inevitable use as a car park, the building was reincarnated in 1986 as the G-Mex Centre. Exhibitions, sporting events and concerts are now staged where once the deafening noise of a lifting safety valve of an impatient steam locomotive was a more familiar sound.
Jim Davenport

Below:
As a former CLC station, a host of ex-LMS and LNER locomotive classes used Manchester Central. Stanier 'Jubilee' 4-6-0s were a familiar sight on London St Pancras workings. One of the last steam duties to use Central was the 8am Buxton-Manchester and return 5.22pm commuter trains, with 'Jubilee' No 45705 *Seahorse* being regularly diagrammed for a time — as on 31 March 1965 — as a reminder of past glories. Note the yellow stripe on the cabside indicating that the engine was banned from running south of Crewe over the electrified lines due to insufficient clearances.
Brian Magilton/Colour-Rail

The first of the 10 Robinson 'Director' Class D10 4-4-0s were introduced in 1913 for top-link duties on the Great Central Railway, but in the 1950s much of their work was confined to ex-CLC routes out of Manchester. Seen on the 60ft turntable at Manchester Central in 1952 is No 62656 *Sir Clement Royds*, while behind is Thompson 'B1' 4-6-0 No 61182 from Gorton shed. Sir Clement Royds was a director of the GCR from 1897 to 1916. The last of the class, No 62653 *Sir Edward Fraser*, was withdrawn in October 1955, No 62656 having been condemned in January of that year. *W. Oliver/Colour-Rail*

Right:

During the 1960s the extensive 20-road Trafford Park shed, coded 9E from May 1950 apart from a 15-month spell as 17F from January 1957, presented a somewhat dilapidated appearance — six roads by then being roofless. Access was gained from the ex-CLC Manchester-Liverpool route by a spur which ran round the back of the Stretford End of Manchester United's Old Trafford football ground from Trafford Park Junction, the connection also providing a link with the Manchester Ship Canal system.

First used in March 1895 by the Midland and Manchester, Sheffield & Lincolnshire (later Great Central) railways, by the end of the century the Great Northern had also taken over part of the building. In 1950 Trafford Park was responsible for 73 engines, 47 previously owned by the LNER, among them one 'Large Director' and seven 'Director' 4-4-0s, 11 'J10' 0-6-0s and nine 'N5' 0-6-2Ts. On the LMS side nine Compound 4-4-0s and six 'Jubilee' 4-6-0s figured prominently. By 1959 the total had been reduced to 53, only two 'J10s' remaining in residence as a reminder of its former Eastern connection. At this time 13 LMS 2-6-4Ts predominated along with six 'Britannia' Pacifics.

During the mid-1960s Stanier 'Black 5' 4-6-0s inevitably provided the main source of traction and on 1 January 1967 the shed had a stud no less than 26 strong, including No 44888, along with 11 2-6-4Ts and 12 Stanier '8F' 2-8-0s. In the summer of 1965, shortly after its arrival at 9E, No 44888 waits for its tender to be replenished under the coaling conveyor. Note the distinctive lighting support, and the brazier which would be put to good use in frosty weather conditions in keeping the water columns flowing. The shed closed from 4 March 1968. *Keith Sanders*

Right:

Former ROD Class O4/3 2-8-0 No 63766 trudges towards Northwich across the Cheshire plain, near Ashley, with a rake of loose-coupled mineral wagons in 1959. Ex-LNER engines were a common sight along this stretch of line owned by the CLC in pre-Grouping days, locomotives from Northwich and Chester (Northgate) sheds having diagrams, along with those based around Manchester. A Gorton engine from December 1954, No 63766 was taken out of service in September 1962. *J. D. Darby*

Below:
Shortly after its arrival at Warrington (Dallam) shed, code 8B, in March 1965, along with 15 of her sisters displaced by the dieselisation of freight traffic on the Midland main line, BR '9F' 2-10-0 No 92058, running tender-first, powers a load of mineral wagons past the lofty signalbox at Skelton Junction and takes the ex-CLC route towards Glazebrook. The signalman at Skelton controlled a three-way split of the line from Northenden Junction, the nearside tracks leading to Warrington Arpley, while in front of the houses on the left is the line to Northwich via Altrincham. No 92058, a product of Crewe in 1955, moved to Carlisle (Kingmoor) (12A) for the last three months of her revenue-earning life in August 1967, after a brief two-month spell at Speke Junction (8C). *Neville R. Knight*

Right
One of the seemingly never-ending cycle of limestone hoppers, from the quarries at Tunstead in the Peak District, to feed the insatiable demands of the ICI chemical works at Northwich, passes Baguley station, on former CLC metals, on 6 April 1963, behind 1943-built (by the Southern Railway at Eastleigh Works) Stanier '8F' 2-8-0 No 48605. The locomotive is coupled to a Fowler tender. For many years these trains provided regular employment for No 48605 working from Northwich shed (8E) before it moved to Birkenhead (8H) for a couple of months in February 1965, and then to Aintree (8L) for its last 15 months of active life. Meanwhile Baguley station had closed its booking office window on 30 November 1964. *Nigel F. W. Dyckhoff*

Above:
Originally intended for War Department service when built by the North British Locomotive Co in 1942, this Stanier '8F' 2-8-0 was added to LMS stock in 1943 as No 8278. It ended its days at Rose Grove shed at the very end of steam in August 1968. Meanwhile on 28 February 1968 as BR No 48278, while attached to Heaton Mersey shed, it is used to advantage pulling a coal train westbound at Northenden Junction. This is the point where the LNWR line from Cheadle meets the CLC route from Stockport Tiviot Dale. Note the bracket signal for the junction. *Neville Fields*

Right:
Manufactured at Crewe in 1939, Stanier '8F' 2-8-0 No 48115 heads east towards Stockport Tiviot Dale during 1966 with a mixed freight, crossing the River Mersey at the approach to Heaton Mersey. The entrance to the shed, home base of No 48115, is just behind the photographer who is standing on the girder bridge which carried the direct Midland Railway Manchester Central-Chinley, via Disley Tunnel, route over the CLC Northenden Junction-Tiviot Dale line at this point. The rear of the train has just cleared Cheadle Junction where the Midland main line could be gained by the connection to be seen in the left background. *Norman Harrop*

Left:
Situated one mile west of Stockport Tiviot Dale station, Heaton Mersey shed was originally owned by the CLC. Opened in 1889, it was coded 9F for most of its BR days. In 1950 facilities were shared by 36 former LMS and 28 ex-LNER engines, the latter comprising no less than 18 'J10' 0-6-0s together with two 'J39' 0-6-0s, six 'N5' 0-6-2Ts and two 'Large Director' Class D11 4-4-0s Nos 62663 *Prince Albert* and 62665 *Mons*. However, Eastern influence was set to decline and by 1960 the last 'J10' had been moved away. Mainstay on the LMS side throughout the 1950s, and, indeed, until the shed closed on 6 May 1968, were 20 or more Stanier '8F' 2-8-0s. Shortly before the veil was drawn over Heaton Mersey, two '8Fs' stand by the coaling stage, near the top of the yard, on 6 April 1968 — No 48529 on a visit from Edge Hill (8A) and No 48329 on its home patch. Within three months both engines were being prepared for the cutters' torch.
Alan C. Gilbert

19

The unglamorous face of steam, and highlighting the primitive facilities which continued in use at many locations right until steam's demise, is captured in this view within the coaling stage at Heaton Mersey shed on 30 March 1968. The coal had to be shovelled by hand from the wagons, seen on the left, into the skips, ready for tipping over the right-hand side into hungry tenders waiting below. At the far end a member of staff takes a well-earned breather in the fresh air, away from the dusty atmosphere that was ever-present when work was in progress. *Neville R. Knight*

Ivatt's last design for the LMS was a rather austere looking, if functional, Class 4 2-6-0. Only three of the type had emerged from Horwich prior to Nationalisation on 1 January 1948. In all 162 were produced, Darlington and Doncaster also laying frames for the class. By May 1964 14 had graduated to Heaton Mersey with a further three down the road at Trafford Park.

Here an unkempt No 43013 canters by nonchalantly near Heaton Mersey on 17 October 1964 with the two-coach 12.10pm SO Manchester Central-Cheadle Heath service. This was hardly a taxing load for the nominal 24,170lb tractive effort available. No 43013 was withdrawn from Heaton Mersey in October 1965 while six of her sisters soldiered on into 1968. The Cheadle Heath locals finished from 2 January 1967, the stations at Chorlton-cum-Hardy and Didsbury, as well as Cheadle Heath, shutting their doors at the same time. *Brian Magilton*

Above:
In the 1950s the ex-GCR Class J10 0-6-0s were a familiar sight on the south side of Manchester, but life's work had not long to run for No 65178, a Pollitt example with larger bearings and a larger tender than as first introduced by Parker in 1892, when photographed in a rural setting at Disley on 11 June 1957. The engine was withdrawn during the autumn of 1959. *W. Oliver/Colour-Rail*

Right:
LMS '4F' 0-6-0 No 44050 draws a train of loose-coupled 16-ton mineral wagons out of the loop at the east end of the 3,866yd-long Disley Tunnel, along the 1902-opened Midland Railway route between New Mills South Junction and Heaton Mersey, on 29 July 1958. The train had been recessed here so as not to impede the passage of a London St Pancras-Manchester express hauled by a Compound 4-4-0 piloting Kentish Town (14B) 'Jubilee' 4-6-0 No 45579 *Punjab*. At the time No 44050 was shedded at Rowsley, and was condemned during autumn 1959. *Neville Fields*

Below:
A clear path ahead for 'Royal Scot' Class 7P 4-6-0 No 46132 *The King's Regiment Liverpool* during its two-year stay at Kentish Town (14B). The locomotive is seen passing the entrance to the goods loop on the approach to Disley Tunnel with a St Pancras-Manchester Central train in 1960. Outshopped by the North British Locomotive Co in 1927 and first named *Phoenix*, No 46132 was rebuilt with a taper-boiler in November 1943. It was withdrawn from Carlisle (Kingmoor) (12A) in February 1964. *W. Oliver/Colour-Rail*

Right:
The driver of Rowsley (17D)-based LMS '4F' 0-6-0 No 44556

keeps a firm grip on the brake descending the 1 in 87 approach to New Mills South Junction with a northbound rake of empties on 15 June 1957. On the left another lengthy mixed freight, which had started from Gowhole Sidings, the leading wagons laden with coal, makes its way towards Manchester. Gowhole Sidings were set in a delightfully rural location, just south of this point, with marshalling facilities on both up and down sides, a prodigious amount of traffic being handled daily, traffic which converged and departed in all directions from this one-time Midland Railway stronghold. Sorting finished in 1969, whilst No 44556 had already been rendered surplus to requirements when withdrawn in December 1963.
W. Oliver/Colour-Rail

The steam age bequeathed the small north Derbyshire village of Chinley with a station far in excess of its status, having five platform faces and an east end bay, needed for the considerable amount of interchange traffic that developed between the former Midland Railway lines which radiated south, north and east. Even some Manchester Central-St Pancras services stopped here, including the route's flagship 'The Palatine' in the up direction, while a turntable was available for the benefit of locomotives on terminating trains. A considerable volume of freight also passed through and, on 22 October 1957, ex-LNWR Class 7F 0-8-0 No 49398 of Speke Junction (8C) clatters past on the eastern approach to the station with a long link of empty coal wagons in tow. No 49398 was withdrawn in November 1959. *W. Oliver/Colour-Rail*

Between 1942 and 1952 no less than 410 of the versatile Thompson 'B1' 4-6-0s were constructed, 340 being ordered from the private locomotive builders North British (290) and Vulcan Foundry (50), while Darlington Works produced 60 and Gorton 10. They were once a common sight around Manchester, particularly on former LNER-operated lines — in early BR days Gorton (39A) had a dozen or more on its register. Later they infiltrated other areas and for a time could be seen on the Hope Valley route to Sheffield. On

11 April 1964 North British example No 61313 was domiciled at the former Midland Canklow shed, near Rotherham (then coded 41D), and is seen making a gutsy departure from Chinley with the 12.55pm all-stations service to Sheffield Midland. The train provided connections at Chinley with both the 11.45am from Manchester Central via Romiley and the 12.25pm Manchester Central-St Pancras. No 61313 ran its last in 1965. *Brian Magilton*

Below:
A light load for a 'Jubilee'! With a strong southwesterly wind blowing across the Peak District, Crewe-built Stanier 4-6-0 No 45618 *New Hebrides*, of Trafford Park shed, is about to take the Sheffield line at Chinley North Junction with a three-coach local from Chinley in 1954. Just discernible is the tender of Stanier '8F' 2-8-0 No 48046 awaiting the road to Tunstead, on the Derby line, with a train of empty ICI limestone hoppers from Northwich.
W. Oliver/Colour-Rail

Right:
Buxton shed's Stanier '8F' 2-8-0 No 48532 slogs over the summit at Peak Forest with a heavy freight from Gowhole Yard to Buxton on 15 February 1968. The engine still seems to have plenty of steam after an arduous seven-mile climb, much of it at 1 in 90, and belying the fact that the locomotive was in its last month of active life before withdrawal. No 48532 was built in the LNER workshops at Doncaster in 1945, and spent its first months on loan to that company before moving to the LMS prior to Nationalisation. Most steam workings in the area finished two weeks later with the closure of Buxton (9L) shed. *John S. Whiteley*

In mid-summer 1958 Trafford Park shed received an allocation of six 'Britannia' Pacifics, mainly for use on Manchester Central-St Pancras trains pending dieselisation. These trains were to take on an increasing importance during the electrification of the rival West Coast route out of Manchester London Road. The shed gained Nos 70004 *William Shakespeare* and 70014 *Iron Duke* from Stewarts Lane (73A), 70015 *Apollo*, 70017 *Arrow* and 70021 *Morning Star* from Cardiff (Canton) (86C), and 70042 *Lord Roberts* from Stratford (30A). On 4 June 1960 the former 'Golden Arrow' regular No 70004 approaches Great Rocks Junction, in the Peak District, with the 2.25pm St Pancras-Manchester Central service. *Alan C. Gilbert*

Trafford Park three-cylinder Compound 4-4-0 No 41163, built in 1925, steps smartly across the four-arch viaduct at the south end of New Mills Tunnel with a local service from Manchester Central to Chinley on 26 March 1957. The train had travelled via Stockport Tiviot Dale. *W. Oliver/Colour-Rail*

Left:
Stone terraces overlook the station at Hayfield, although the caravan looks a little incongruous, as BR Swindon-built Class 3 2-6-2T No 82003 waits to return down the three-mile branch to New Mills Central bunker-first with the LCGB 'Cotton Spinner' railtour on 16 April 1966. A design not familiar to Manchester prior to April 1965, when Patricroft shed gained five ex-Western Region examples, including the prototype No 82000 and No 82003. All had previously worked on the Cambrian lines from Machynlleth shed during the early 1960s. The quintet at Patricroft were all taken out of traffic during the autumn of 1966.

During the 1950s Hayfield enjoyed a through service of 15 trains daily to Manchester London Road, with one extra on Saturdays. There were eight trains on Sundays. Despite the advent of DMUs in 1957 the branch closed completely from 5 January 1970. The trackbed was subsequently purchased by Derbyshire County Council in 1973 and converted to form the Sett Valley Trail, a pleasant walk along this former Midland and Great Central Joint line where, unfortunately, one can now only imagine the passing of the ex-GC 'C13' and 'C14' 4-4-2Ts which once reigned supreme in these Derbyshire hills. *Richard S. Greenwood*

Left:
The pride of Derby (17A) shed, 'Patriot' class 4-6-0 No 45509 *The Derbyshire Yeomanry* rides high above the River Goyt, along the impressive Marple Viaduct, with a four-coach local for Manchester Central in 1953. Out of sight to the right is the aqueduct carrying the Peak Forest Canal, while in the distance can be glimpsed Marple Wharf Junction signalbox, along with the signals controlling the routes to Chinley and Macclesfield. No 45509 saw out the last three years of its 28-year working life at Newton Heath shed, arriving there in August 1958. *Eric Oldham/Colour-Rail*

With clouds gathering in the distance over the Peak District, former GCR Class C13 4-4-2T No 67403 runs bunker first on the approach to Romiley, soon after crossing Marple Viaduct, with a Macclesfield Central-Manchester London Road all-stations service in 1953. Note the distant bracket signal arms indicating that after the Romiley stop the train will take the Hyde route to Manchester. This 22-mile route to Macclesfield, as opposed to the 17$\frac{1}{2}$ miles via Stockport, was closed beyond Rose Hill (Marple) on 5 January 1970. The line from Marple Wharf Junction was in the joint ownership of the GCR and North Staffordshire Railway in pre-Grouping days. No 67403 was withdrawn during April 1955. *Eric Oldham/Colour-Rail*

On its last diagram working from Speke Junction (8C), Riddles '9F' 2-10-0 No 92160 powers its final load of Yorkshire-mined coal bound for Merseyside through Apethorne Junction, between Hyde and Woodley, just coming off the line from Godley Junction, on 4 May 1968. The wagons had been hauled through Woodhead Tunnel by a Class EM1 Bo-Bo electric locomotive (later Class 76). In all, 251 '9Fs' were built by BR between 1954 and 1960 — numerically the largest of the Standard classes. No 92160 was a product of Crewe Works in 1957. On closure of Speke shed to steam two days later, No 92160 travelled north to Carnforth (10A), where it was one of the last two condemned by BR in June 1968. *Brian Magilton*

Right:
The 125-ton bulk of Heaton Mersey-allocated Stanier '8F' 2-8-0 No 48319 is swung round by the crew on the turntable at Godley Junction, prior to running west with yet more coal transported across the Pennines from Yorkshire via the electrified Woodhead route on 17 April 1968. In the background a sister locomotive is engaged on similar duties, while in the distance the high-rise flats of Hattersley stand like sentinels amidst the landscape. *Brian Magilton*

Left:
The single-track steeply-graded Waterside branch — over ³/₄-mile was at 1 in 40 — was opened by the Manchester, Sheffield & Lincolnshire Railway in 1879 to serve local industry. It left the Woodhead route at Old Dinting, between Broadbottom and Dinting. Treading the branch in June 1959 is 'Pom Pom' Class J11 0-6-0 No 64311 with a local pick-up goods, the engine sporting a 9G (Gorton) shedplate. At the time Gorton had 25 of this Robinson-designed class, introduced on the GCR in 1901, on its books. No 64311 was designated as scrap in January 1961, while the Waterside branch closed on 2 March 1964. *W. Oliver/Colour-Rail*

Below:
Former ROD member of the Class O4 2-8-0 family No 63870, built with steam brake only and no water scoop, plods by Hyde Junction, eastbound towards Yorkshire, with a long string of wooden-bodied wagons in 1952. In 1950 Gorton shed had over 50 of these purposeful locomotives for use on heavy freight traffic and, prior to electrification in 1954 (the catenary for which was already in place at Hyde), examples based at sheds on both sides of the Pennines were a regular sight on the long climb to Woodhead Tunnel. No 63870 was a Langwith Junction (40E) engine, and continued in service until November 1961. *W. Oliver/Colour-Rail*

The Class C13 4-4-2Ts were a Robinson GCR design, first built at Gorton in 1903 for intensive suburban work. Eight of the 40-strong class were push-pull fitted and one such, No 67438, here propels a couple of coaches, forming a train from Manchester London Road, past Hyde Junction towards Hadfield, in 1952. The class had over 50 years of association with Gorton shed, the last survivor (No 67417) being withdrawn from the shed during the four weeks ending 13 February 1960.
W. Oliver/Colour-Rail

Right:
William Stanier's first design for the LMS
following his appointment as CME was a
taper-boilered Mogul for mixed traffic. The
first of the class appeared in 1933. While
often seen in the area, members of the 40-
strong class were never allocated in any
numbers to the Manchester area until early
December 1964 when five were drafted to
Gorton, followed by a further 10 a month
later. At the time of its closure in June 1965
Gorton had become responsible for no less
than 19 of the 26 survivors, which were then
transferred *en masse* to Heaton Mersey.
No 42954 was the final one, being
withdrawn in February 1967. Approaching
Guide Bridge station westbound with a
freight on 28 December 1963 is No 42948,
just recently reallocated from Stoke &
Cockshute (5D) to Springs Branch (Wigan)
(8F), but later to join the Gorton fleet at the
end of May 1965. *Brian Magilton*

Right:
Seen at work during its final 12 months in
capital stock on 7 November 1964,
Warrington (Dallam)-based three-cylinder
'Jubilee' class 4-6-0 No 45655 *Keith*
cautiously hauls a mixed freight off the
former LNWR line from Stockport towards
Guide Bridge station. The ex-GCR route to
Manchester Piccadilly (formerly London
Road) lies straight ahead behind the
locomotive. *Brian Magilton*

Gorton was a massive shed, coded 39A, under Eastern Region control in early BR days, with an allocation of over 160 ex-LNER type locomotives, composed of 11 different classes, in 1950. Moreover, the depot had, for short periods of time, the use of engines which were there for running-in purposes following a visit to the adjacent locomotive works, before being despatched to their home sheds.

Situated in the heart of London Midland Region territory it was only a matter of time before its loyalty to its LNER antecedence would be challenged and, following the closure of the nearby ex-Midland Railway Belle Vue (26F) shed on 16 April 1956, 10 ex-LMSR locomotives were reallocated to Gorton. Then from February 1958, as part of some wholesale regional boundary changes, the shed was placed under LM management. Initially it was coded 9H, but this was amended within weeks to 9G, which was retained until closure. By 1959 little had seemingly changed, for, of the 113 locomotives based there, 95 were of LNER extraction. But, by October 1963, just three Thompson 'B1' 4-6-0s remained of the old order — Nos 61039 *Steinbok*, 61269 and 61369. Shortly afterwards the LM takeover was complete.

On 4 April 1965 LM influence is apparent with both Hughes/Fowler and Stanier 2-6-0 and Stanier '8F' 2-8-0 designs in view. The shed closed on 14 June 1965. *Neville Fields*

Right:
Gorton Works, known as 'The Tank', was founded by the Manchester, Sheffield & Lincolnshire Railway in 1848, and constructed 1,006 locomotives. The last locomotives to be built there were a batch of 10 Thompson 'B1' 4-6-0s for BR in 1948 and 1949. Waiting to return to traffic after overhaul on 18 September 1960 is Colwick-allocated Robinson Class O4 2-8-0 No 63816, a type with a long affiliation to Gorton as the Works built 117 of the class. In January 1959 the Works passed from Eastern to LMR control and, whilst it continued to deal mainly with ex-LNER engines along with ex-WD 2-8-0s and BR '9F' 2-10-0s, it was perhaps ironic that the last locomotive repaired was ex-LMS '8F' 2-8-0 No 48520 in April 1963. The Works became defunct the following month.
J. G. Dewing/Colour-Rail

Below right:
Against a backcloth of terraced houses, Stanier Class 5 4-6-0 No 45339, constructed at Newcastle-upon-Tyne by Armstrong Whitworth in 1937, hauls the Newton Heath breakdown crane between Ashton-under-Lyne and Stalybridge on 12 March 1965.

These versatile machines, referred to by some local trainspotters as 'Mickeys', were a very common sight in and around Manchester on a wide variety of tasks from the mid-1930s — the first left the production line in 1934 — right until the end of the steam era. The class ultimately totalled 842, the last two not being released from Horwich until 1951. In 1950 94 were maintained at the area's sheds, which included: 36 at Patricroft, 31 at Newton Heath and 17 at Longsight. On 1 January 1967 no less than 99 were on the registers and, while Patricroft had none, Newton Heath still had 30, Trafford Park had 26 and Stockport (Edgeley) 17. The other 26 were divided equally between Bolton and Heaton Mersey. At the start of 1968 62 remained active. *Brian Magilton*

Stanier 'Black 5' 4-6-0 No 44696 graced Manchester area sheds throughout its existence. Despatched new to Newton Heath in December 1950, as one of a batch of 10 built at Horwich experimentally fitted with Timken roller bearings to the driving axles only, it remained there until withdrawn in May 1967, apart from a seven-month spell at Trafford Park from February 1964, followed by nine months at Stockport (Edgeley). During its comparatively short sojourn away from Newton Heath No 44696 approaches Stalybridge from Stockport with a mixed rake of freight vehicles, having followed the Hooley Hill route, which bypassed the Guide Bridge complex, on 12 September 1964. *Brian Magilton*

Built at Derby in 1954, Patricroft-allocated BR Standard Class 5 4-6-0 No 73053 storms through Mossley, on the 15-mile climb from Manchester to Diggle, with the summer SO 8.25am Manchester Victoria-Scarborough service on 8 July 1967. The train's reporting number — 1N73 — is prominently chalked on the smokebox door. No 73053 had spells at Leeds (Holbeck), Neasden, Woodford Halse and Shrewsbury before arriving at Patricroft in July 1965. It was taken out of service in March 1968. *Brian Magilton*

One of the BR 'Britannia' class 4-6-2s based at Stockport (Edgeley), No 70026 *Polar Star*, powers past Greenfield Junction with a Stockport-Leeds parcels train on 25 October 1966. Clearly seen are the hand-holds on the smoke deflectors which were cut following an accident which befell No 70026 at Milton, near Didcot, in November 1955 while working a Treherbert-London Paddington excursion. At the same time the original handrails were removed. Other Western Region 'Britannias' were similarly modified in an effort to improve the forward vision from the cab. Lack of forward vision had been seen as a contributory factor in the 1955 accident. *Polar Star* was retired in January 1967 after a comparatively short working life of only 14 years and three months. On the right can be seen the remains of the line which ran down to Oldham Clegg Street, which was closed to passengers on 2 May 1955 and to goods from 13 April 1964. *Don Cash*

A reminder that in the east of the region winters can be hard and long as a blanket of snow covers Lees in March 1954 — indeed the enginemen at Lees shed were often called upon for snow clearing duties. Here Fowler Class 3 2-6-2T No 40059 leaves Lees on its 6¾-mile journey from Oldham Clegg Street to Delph, a service popularly known as the 'Delph Donkey'. Prior to its closure to passengers on 2 May 1955 13 trains left Delph on weekdays bound for Oldham together with one that ran as far as Greenfield only. There were an additional five trains on Saturdays. Goods traffic continued on the branch until 4 November 1963. *Jim Davenport*

Lees shed, Oldham, variously coded 26F, 26E and 9P by BR, usually had a fleet of about 20 engines during the 1950s. In May 1952, before the building was reroofed, examples of three of the four classes it maintained in the early 1950s rest in the shed yard — Aspinall L&YR '3F' 0-6-0 No 52365, with an unidentified WD 'Austerity' 2-8-0 behind, along with Fowler Class 3 2-6-2T No 40012. Missing from this view is a member of the fourth class allocated at this time, a Fowler ex-LMS '7F' 0-8-0. This former LNWR depot closed on 13 April 1964.
Jim Davenport/Colour-Rail

During its last full year of service, on 27 June 1963, before withdrawal the following spring, rebuilt 'Royal Scot' Class 7P 4-6-0 No 46136 *The Border Regiment*, of Carlisle (Upperby) (12B), drifts down the 1 in 59/47 Miles Platting bank at the approach to Manchester Victoria with the summer-dated 11am SO from Filey Holiday Camp. Built in 1927 by the North British Locomotive Co and originally named *Goliath*, No 46136 was rebuilt with a taper-boiler and double chimney in 1950. On the right a 1,200V dc EMU (later Class 504) nears journey's end forming a train from Bury Bolton Street. *Brian Magilton*

Left:
On 9 May 1964 Hughes/Fowler 'Crab' 2-6-0 No 42716 and Stanier 'Jubilee' 4-6-0 No 45574 *India* have just drawn to a halt amidst the gloomy smoke-ridden confines of Manchester Victoria with a troop special (reporting number 1X23). Victoria was the Lancashire & Yorkshire Railway's main station in the city, with a history dating back to 1844.
Brian Magilton

Right:
Following continuing disquiet over its arrangements with the L&YR for the use of Victoria, the LNWR opened its own station nearby in June 1884 and, although actually in Salford, was always known as Manchester Exchange. Its overall roof compared favourably with the other principal stations in the city, and is seen here forming a backdrop for work-stained 'Britannia' Pacific No 70027 *Rising Star* departing with a Llandudno train in June 1963. When new in September 1952 No 70027 was allocated to the Western Region, arriving on the LMR in July 1962. Initially allocated by the LMR to Aston (21D), it moved to Holyhead (6J) in May 1963. It was withdrawn in June 1967.
Brian Magilton

Above:

Salford, even though a city in its own right, the Roman Catholic cathedral being not far from the station, has always been overshadowed by its more illustrious neighbour Manchester. Indeed it almost seemed an afterthought that a 'Princess Coronation' class Pacific was named *City of Salford*, the last in line, No 46257, in 1948, whilst Manchester was so honoured by No 46246 in 1943.

In keeping, the ex-L&YR station in Salford was rather basic in comparison to its Manchester counterparts, and was served mainly by trains from Southport, the Fylde Coast and East Lancashire on their way to Victoria. The LNWR, whose line to Manchester Exchange passed alongside the south side of the station, never provided any platforms at this point. However, at peak times the station would be thronged (and still is), as many business people and shoppers found it more convenient for their places of work or for the department stores on Deansgate, rather than Victoria itself.

On 27 June 1964 Springs Branch (Wigan) (8F)-based Stanier two-cylinder 2-6-4T No 42601, with a cylinder drain cock open as it passes the platform end signalbox, heads towards home with a Manchester Victoria-Wigan Wallgate stopping train. No 42601 was withdrawn the following year after a life of 29 years, having been assembled by the North British Locomotive Co, Glasgow, in 1936. *Brian Magilton*

Right:

Standing at the primitive coaling stage facility amidst the sprawling Irwell Street Goods Yard, Salford, ex-L&YR Aspinall Class 21 0-4-0ST No 51232, constructed in 1906 to a design of 1891, awaits its next call of duty during April 1963. Agecroft shed was responsible for providing shunters for the yard, engines normally being on hand continuously from early Monday morning until they returned home to the main depot on Saturday afternoon. No 51232 was one of the last 'Pugs' to work the yard before breaking an axle the following month, an event which precipitated its withdrawal. *Don Cash*

During 1968 BR Standard Class 5 4-6-0 No 73069 achieved fame through a number of appearances on enthusiasts' specials. It survived to become the last of the class in service and was marked for scrap only after steam's finale in August 1968. Earlier that year

No 73069 has a more mundane task leading a convoy of vans off the connection with the Manchester Ship Canal system at Eccles. *Frank Cronin*

Right:

The LNWR commissioned the original eight-road Patricroft shed in 1885 but, with space at a premium, a second 10-road building was added at right angles some 20 years later. Throughout the 1950s over 70 engines were maintained at the depot. Patricroft was coded 10C until 1958, then 26F before becoming 9H in 1963.

On a visit from Carlisle (Upperby) (12B), one of the 10 Fowler 'Patriot' class three-cylinder 4-6-0s never to carry a name, No 45544, poses in the yard outside the old shed on 22 August 1959. Also in the picture are two BR Standard Class 5 4-6-0s — with No 73040 on the right — representing a class that became synonymous with Patricroft in later years. First to arrive were Nos 73023 and 73024, sent new from Derby in November 1951, and by November 1966 no less than 42 had congregated at the depot out of a total allocation of 63, the others being 16 Stanier '8F' 2-8-0s and five BR Standard Class 3 2-6-2Ts. The shed closed on 1 July 1968.
K. C. H. Fairey

Right:

Stanier Class 5 4-6-0 No 44888 crosses Chat Moss along tracks opened in 1830 by the Liverpool & Manchester Railway, with the first leg of a Roch Valley Railway Society double return Manchester-Southport excursion, which utilised various routes to the coast on 21 July 1968. It was fitting that some of the last steam-hauled trains should follow this route, as did the final valedictory special of all from Liverpool Lime Street to Carlisle on 11 August 1968 — the line standing as a tribute to George Stephenson who faced much opposition, even ridicule, at planning a railway over this four-mile expanse of unstable peat moss. His solution of effectively floating the rails across on a brushwood foundation has stood the test of time. No 44888 was built at Crewe in 1945.
Jim Winkley

Above:

The foundations of Atherton Bag Lane station lay alongside the historic Bolton & Leigh Railway, the first section of which was opened in 1828. The regular passenger service from Bolton Great Moor Street to Kenyon Junction, which served Bag Lane, finished on 29 March 1954 and, following the discontinuance of Wakes Weeks specials from Bolton to North Wales after 1959, it became strictly freight only — until January 1969 when the last section north of Howe Bridge was closed.

During the last years the principal traffic was the conveyance of raw materials to a steelworks at Hulton's Sidings, just north of Chequerbent, which involved a tortuous climb from Atherton, officially at 1 in 30, but even more demanding in places due to colliery subsidence. It was often necessary to split trains at Atherton and take them forward in stages and even then the help of a banker was needed — Patricroft shed usually providing the motive power.

Observed from the remains of Atherton Bag Lane station on 19 April 1968 Stanier '8F' 2-8-0 No 48775 prepares for the ordeal ahead, while sister engine No 48212 stands ready to attach a brake-van to the rear wagon and provide the necessary assistance to Hulton's Sidings. *Brian Magilton*

Right:

Emitting a cataclysm of sound, while utilising every available ounce of the 64,880lb of tractive effort nominally available, another pair of Stanier '8F' 2-8-0s, No 48327 leading and No 48529 at the back, combine forces to lift another heavy load up the taxing incline to Chequerbent from Atherton on 31 May 1968. *Neville Fields*

An island platform serving only the slow lines were a feature at a number of stations on the former L&YR direct Manchester-Wigan Wallgate via Atherton Central route. On 28 May 1966 Stanier 'Black 5' 4-6-0 No 44679, one of eight built at Horwich in 1950 experimentally fitted with Skefco roller bearings, approaches Walkden High Level with a Prescot-Swinton (next-but-one station after Walkden) special, for a Rugby League Championship Final between St Helens and Halifax. Passengers later rode home behind No 44679 in joyful mood — St Helens having won 35-12. It will be noted by the rusty nature of the rails on the left that the fast lines were already out of use pending lifting. Until March 1954 Walkden was served also by a Low Level station on the ex-LNWR Manchester-Bolton Great Moor Street line. *Alan C. Gilbert*

Fowler ex-LMS '7F' inside-cylindered 0-8-0 No 49511, built at Crewe in 1929 and looking a bit the worse for wear, rests in the yard at the former L&YR Agecroft shed in 1958, buffered-up to Aspinall L&YR Class 2F 0-6-0ST No 51458. While No 49511 was a Newton Heath engine, Agecroft had its own allocation of these lumbering work-horses for heavy freight diagrams and which, for some seemingly inexplicable reason, were generally known as 'Austin Sevens'. The last four of this once 175-strong class were based at Agecroft in 1961.

In the 1950s Agecroft had over 50 engines of ex-LMS and ex-WD power to call on, including 16 Hughes/Fowler 'Crab' 2-6-0s in 1956. A surprise at the end of the decade was the drafting in of five Thompson 'B1' class 4-6-0s, among them the named No 61008 *Kudu*, only for these to be replaced in 1962 by a batch of Stanier 'Jubilee' 4-6-0s — the most notable type to carry the 26B shed code. The depot was taken out of use on 22 October 1966, the shedplates having been amended to 9J in 1963. *RCTS/Colour-Rail*

Left:
An interloper at Newton Heath on 21 October 1965, ex-LNER
Gresley 'A4' Pacific No 60007 *Sir Nigel Gresley* positively gleams
amidst the more regular fare for the shed, Stanier Class 5 4-6-0
No 45055, on a visit from Southport (8M), being prominent on the
left. The Pacific was on shed prior to hauling an A4 Preservation
Society special from Manchester to London Paddington via Chester,
which set out on a typical autumnal misty morning two days later.
No 60007 had travelled light engine from its Scottish home at
Aberdeen (Ferryhill) (61B). *Don Cash*

Above:
The huge 24-road through shed at Newton Heath, the erstwhile 26A
until September 1963 and then 9D, was opened by the L&YR in
1876. In 1950 it boasted the largest locomotive fleet in Manchester
— 167, one more than Gorton — including 32 ex-L&YR designs of
three different classes. In 1959 16 L&YR engines remained at a time
when the shed still possessed 159 steam locomotives on its duty
lists. From the mid-1930s 26A had the use of a selection of 'Jubilee'
4-6-0s for express passenger work, while in the 1960s
representatives of the 'Royal Scot' and 'Britannia' classes joined the
fold. In 1959 the heavy freight diagrams were catered for by 25 ex-
WD 2-8-0s and 10 BR '9F' 2-10-0s along with six Fowler '7F'
0-8-0s.

On a showery 22 June 1968, with just over a week remaining
before the fires were extinguished for the last time, Stanier
smokeboxes face each other across the front of the shed. During
1968 Newton Heath relied solely on Stanier tender engines, 20
'Black 5' 4-6-0s and 17 '8F' 2-8-0s being resident at the start of the
year. *Chris Banks*

Manufactured by the North British Locomotive Co in 1942, Stockport (Edgeley)'s Stanier '8F' 2-8-0 No 48182 enters Mumps yard, Oldham, with a lengthy load of empty parcels vans on 28 February 1968.

In all, 852 of these powerful heavy freight locomotives were built over 11 years from 1935, many for the War Department, with some going overseas, while in 1959 BR owned 666. They were very familiar to the Manchester railway observer, 64 being located in the area in 1950 spread between seven sheds and, while numbers had been reduced to 40 in 1959, numbers had increased to 104 by 1 January 1967. Heaton Mersey had 26 with Bolton, Newton Heath, Patricroft, Stockport (Edgeley) and Trafford Park all having a dozen or more. At the start of steam's last year, 76 remained, dispersed between the same six sheds, out of 150 still at work. *Don Cash*

A tradition of the Lancashire mill towns was the annual Wakes Week holiday — later extended to a fortnight — when, with the factories closed except for maintenance work, seemingly half the population emigrated temporarily. Umpteen specials would be provided to cater for the exodus to such places as Blackpool, Llandudno and Rhyl, while the more intrepid set out for the South Coast or the West Country. A similar number of trains would be required the following week to return the holidaymakers home.

Following the very intensive operation that took place each weekend during the summers of the 1950s, when resources were stretched to the limit, the number of specials declined over the next decade due to various factors. Not least, more and more people were beginning to enjoy the benefit of a family car, while continental holidays were becoming increasingly attractive and, also, many employers introduced a staggered holiday pattern which lessened the impact of the Wakes Week locally. Further, Dr Beeching had decreed that it was totally uneconomic to maintain hundreds of carriages for just a few outings each year.

Even so in 1966 the Fylde Coast remained a popular destination for some Wakes Week revellers who relied on BR for transport and, on 18 June, Newton Heath turned out Ivatt Class 2 2-6-0 No 46412 and Stanier Class 5 4-6-0 No 45339 (the train engine carrying the reporting code) to head an Oldham-Blackpool holiday special. The train is seen at Heyside, between Royton and Shaw, cantering towards Rochdale. The Ivatt was on one of its last outings before withdrawal. *Don Cash*

Despite being only three months away from being towed to the scrap line, Riddles BR Standard Class 9F 2-10-0 No 92075 still appears sturdy and in good heart, even if somewhat unkempt, while heading towards Oldham, at Heyside, with a freight on 18 June 1966. Initially No 92075 worked from Doncaster (36A), on the Eastern Region, after manufacture at Crewe in February 1956. It was transferred to Annesley (38B) a year later. From February 1958 the engine became part of LMR stock when that depot was placed under LMR control and stayed in the East Midlands until its final move to Carlisle (Kingmoor) (12A) at the end of March 1966. After only $10^1/_2$ years of active service it was condemned in September 1966. *Don Cash*

With the Pennine foothills behind, and despite nearing the end of its 30-year existence, Stanier 'Jubilee' class three-cylinder 4-6-0 No 45623 *Palestine*, of Newton Heath shed, makes a rapturous departure from New Hey, between Rochdale and Oldham, with a football special *en route* to Stockport on 23 March 1963. *Palestine* was deleted from capital stock in July 1964. *Richard S. Greenwood*

Left:
With Milnrow station in the background, Aintree (27B)-based Horwich 'Crab' 2-6-0 No 42721 has charge of a short mixed freight from Bolton to Royton Junction, which had travelled via Bury and Rochdale, on 26 May 1961. Before moving to Merseyside in March 1957, No 42721 was an Agecroft engine. It returned to Agecroft in September 1963 for the last month of its active life. It had also been based at Wigan, Bolton and Lancaster (Green Ayre) sheds in the interim. *Richard S. Greenwood*

Below left:
To assist the war effort Riddles designed for the Ministry of Supply a powerful 2-8-0 that was basic yet functional and easy to maintain. A total of 935 were constructed from 1943 to 1945, 545 by the North British Locomotive Co and 390 by Vulcan Foundry. Many were shipped overseas — some never returning — while later BR, realising their worth for heavy freight haulage, purchased 533 to add to the 200 previously bequeathed by the LNER at Nationalisation.

With the safety-valves lifting, Wakefield (56A) stalwart No 90417, fitted with a snow plough, drifts towards Rochdale on 1 January 1963. The locomotive was built by North British in March 1945 as WD No 78551 and returned from France in 1947. The train, passing Belfield, has carried coal from Yorkshire across the Pennines on the Calder Valley route. Known to many as a 'Dub-Dee' and to some as a 'Bed Iron', No 90417 severed its Wakefield connection in October 1966 when it moved to Sunderland (52G), and thus ended its regular forays into Lancashire after 16 years on these turns. It was withdrawn the following summer. *Richard S. Greenwood*

Chartered brake-van specials for enthusiasts over lines not normally open to passengers were a regular feature of the 1960s. One such special on 19 February 1967, jointly sponsored by the Roch Valley Railway Society and the Locomotive Club of Great Britain, made three return trips between Rochdale and Whitworth behind Aspinall L&YR Class 21 0-4-0ST No 51218 of 1901 vintage. The train is seen here crossing Healey Dell Viaduct.

While many of her classmates never strayed far from their original 'Lanky' pastures, No 51218 led a somewhat nomadic and, indeed, charmed existence. For much of the 1950s it was based at Crewe South (5B), but following a spell at Widnes (8D) it was transferred to the Western Region in September 1959. Three years were spent at Bristol (Barrow Road) (82E), before a move to Swansea East Dock (87D) and then Neath (87A) from where it was withdrawn during the autumn of 1964 as the last surviving ex-L&YR engine in capital stock. Fortunately it was to be rescued from oblivion by the L&Y Saddletanks Fund. Since withdrawal, No 51218 has normally been resident on the Keighley & Worth Valley Railway.

Passenger services on the Rochdale-Bacup line ended on 16 June 1947 and by the time of this photograph goods traffic had been cut back to Whitworth — the branch closing completely on 21 August 1967. Today one can walk part of the route, including this section over the towering eight-arch Healey Dell Viaduct, which together with a conventional metal bridge spanning a minor road at the south end, now form part of a nature trail. But, oh for the sound of steam at this secluded spot not far from the bustle of Rochdale itself!
Derek Huntriss

The driver and fireman prepare to replenish the tanks of Stanier taper-boilered 2-6-4T No 42616 at Rochdale on 1 July 1967 before returning home to Low Moor shed (56F) light engine. The engine had arrived at the head of the terminating early evening parcels train from Bradford Exchange. Note the fine array of semaphore signals controlling the east end of the station, together with the water columns.

The LMS ordered 206 of the Stanier-designed two-cylinder version of the 2-6-4Ts from 1935; No 42616 came from the North British Locomotive Co, which was responsible for 73 of the class in total, in 1937. The remainder were built at Derby, with deliveries being completed in 1943. No 42616 was the final member of the class in service, being withdrawn with the closure of Low Moor shed on 2 October 1967. *Richard S. Greenwood*

The encroaching late evening gloom at Rochdale is brightened by a most unusual visitor, rebuilt three-cylinder 'B16/3' 4-6-0 No 61434 of York (50A) on 23 July 1963. It was working home on the 8.40pm Rochdale-Normanton parcels service. Earlier this former North Eastern Railway locomotive, released to traffic from Darlington in 1922 and rebuilt by BR in 1949 with individual sets of Walschaerts valve gear for each cylinder in place of the original Stephenson gear as installed by Raven, had passed through Rochdale assisting a 'Black 5' on the Newcastle-Manchester Red Bank empty vans service. Note the scorched smokebox door.
Richard S. Greenwood

Hughes/Fowler 'Crab' Class 6P5F 2-6-0 No 42708 hustles the Newcastle Scotswood Sidings-Manchester Red Bank empty newspaper vans past the coal yard at Castleton Sidings, 1/4-mile west of Rochdale station, on 16 May 1962. This service was normally double-headed. Introduced in 1926, 245 of these versatile Moguls were built, 70 at Horwich and 175 at Crewe. Manchester sheds had charge of 58 in 1950, 21 at Newton Heath (including No 42708), 19 at Longsight and 14 at Agecroft, with Belle Vue and Stockport (Edgeley) having a couple each. No 42708 transferred its affections to Bolton shed in September 1962 and was withdrawn in July 1964. *Richard S. Greenwood*

During a brief three-month sojourn at Newton Heath shed, Stanier Class 5 4-6-0 No 45103 passes Castleton station southbound, towards Manchester, with a short freight on 30 July 1963. Coming off the production line at Vulcan Foundry, Newton-le-Willows, in 1935, the engine had previously had a long spell at 26A in the 1950s. However, in 1963 it was domiciled at no less than five sheds: Agecroft sending it to Barrow in January, then Carlisle (Kingmoor) keeping it a mere three weeks before its move back to Newton Heath in early July, 26A passing this itinerant 'Black 5' on to Speke Junction in October and Speke, in turn, disposing of it to Edge Hill in January 1964. Perhaps these movements are an indication that the shed foremen were none too impressed by its latter-day performance. No 45103 was made available for tender to the scrap trade the following October, among the first 112 of the class to suffer that fate. *Richard S. Greenwood*

Left:
Just a month short of its three score years and ten, and nearing the end of its active life prior to withdrawal, Aspinall L&YR Class 27 '3F' 0-6-0 No 52129 enjoys a well-earned breather at Castleton yard on 20 May 1961. The class ultimately totalled 450, No 52129 being released to traffic from Horwich in June 1891 as L&YR No 1089, its final shed being Bury (26D). On the right is John Fowler diesel-mechanical 0-4-0 shunter No ED6, a service locomotive based at Castleton Permanent Way Depot.
Richard S. Greenwood/Colour-Rail

Left:
In its last two months of service Bank Hall (27A)-based LMS '2P' 4-4-0 No 40684 takes the Bury line at Castleton East Junction with the 8.40am Rochdale-Liverpool Exchange service on 26 May 1961. During the 1950s Bolton, Longsight and Patricroft sheds had small allocations of these high-stepping machines with 6ft 9in driving wheels.
Richard S. Greenwood

Long-time Bolton shed resident, WD 'Austerity' '8F' 2-8-0 No 90267 (North British-built in October 1943 as WD No 77379 and purchased by BR in December 1948) eases away from Linnyshaw Moss Sidings — which provided a connection with the NCB Walkden system — for the short journey to Kearsley, on the BR Manchester-Bolton line, on 2 September 1964. Great care will be needed by the driver on the 1 in 45 down gradient with no less than 66 wagons and a brake-van in tow. One month later No 90267

severed its ties with the Bolton area, after 11 years, when it was transferred to Merseyside, at Aintree (8L), where it spent its last six months of revenue-earning service before withdrawal in March 1965.

In 1959 there was work for 63 WDs in the Manchester area, eight at both Bolton and Lees sheds, 11 each at Agecroft and Bury, while Newton Heath had 25. By early 1965 all, like No 90267, had moved on to pastures new or the breakers' yard. *Alan C. Gilbert*

The fine lines of Aspinall L&YR Class 5 '2P' 2-4-2T No 50855 are seen to advantage as the locomotive bides time by the coaling tower outside the ex-L&YR Bolton shed in September 1955. In 1950, of a total of 47 locomotives on the Bolton books, 21 were of L&YR pedigree, including nine 2-4-2Ts but, by 1959, only nine ex-L&YR locomotives remained out of a reduced stock of 36. These included just one 2-4-2T No 50850. In addition, the depot could usually call on a number of engines for running-in purposes after overhaul or repair at Horwich Works. No 50855, built in 1900, ran its last in 1958. *T. B. Owen/Colour-Rail*

Following the demise of Bury shed (9M) on 12 April 1965, the Bolton allocation was increased to 57, including eight Ivatt Class 2 2-6-0s previously at Bury. Other well-represented classes were Stanier 'Black 5' 4-6-0s (20), Stanier '8F' 2-8-0s (14) and ex-LMS Class 4 2-6-4Ts (nine), along with three Standard Class 2 2-6-2Ts, a couple of 'Jinty' 0-6-0Ts and LMS '4F' 0-6-0 No 44311. On

29 June 1965 former Bury Ivatt 2-6-0 No 46504 lies at the back of the 12-road Bolton shed, its 9K shedplate still to be fitted. Bolton was perhaps better known as 26C, its code until 1963. Behind is an ex-LMS 2-6-4T and, on the right, Drewry diesel-mechanical 0-6-0 shunter No D2228. The shed closed on 1 July 1968. *Brian Magilton*

The last named train to enjoy steam haulage on BR was the 'Belfast Boat Express' between Manchester Victoria and Heysham Harbour. The first weekend in May 1968 witnessed steam's swansong, when the Stanier 'Black 5s' involved carried a red-backed headboard above the smokebox door in the traditional manner. During its last months, the northbound working in particular became very popular with enthusiasts, so much so that the 'Twenty Fifty-Five Club' (in honour of the departure time from Manchester) was founded to perpetuate its memory and continue the many friendships made on those journeys.

On 17 March 1968 'Black 5' No 45025 pauses at Bolton Trinity Street with the 8.55pm from Manchester, due in Heysham at 10.57pm to provide a connection with the overnight sailing to Belfast. No 45025 came off the production line at Vulcan Foundry, Newton-le-Willows, Lancashire, in August 1934, being withdrawn from its last shed, Carnforth, in August 1968. It remains the oldest surviving Stanier Class 5, the first Vulcan engines preceding the Crewe-built No 45000 by six months, for No 45025 was subsequently purchased privately from BR and is now normally resident on the Strathspey Railway, Aviemore, in the Scottish Highlands. *David C. Rodgers*

In the Manchester area the L&YR provided water troughs at Lostock, west of Bolton, Smithy Bridge, near Rochdale, and Walkden, while the LNWR laid them at Eccles. These were a most useful facility which saved valuable time in engines not having to take water at station stops. However, by the time of this photograph, on 18 May 1968, the troughs at Lostock had been taken out although the pumping house and water tank are still *in situ*. Passing the site, and nearing Lostock Junction, is a Warwickshire Railway Society special making for Blackpool in the capable hands of two Class 5 4-6-0s — Stanier No 44949 leading and BR Standard No 73069. No 44949 was built at nearby Horwich in 1946 and No 73069 at Derby in 1954. *Barrie Walker*

The LMS Class 4 2-6-4Ts, highly regarded by many, first appeared in 1927, the final few of the 645 built not entering service until 1951. They were a ubiquitous breed around Manchester, every shed in the area, except Plodder Lane (10D), having them on the books at some time or other in BR days. In 1950 the Fowler, Stanier and Fairburn derivatives were all represented among the 83 maintained. Newton Heath and Longsight provided a berth for over half with 26 and 17 respectively.

Constructed at Derby in 1946 Fairburn-designed No 42249 spent many years in the London suburbs working from Plaistow and Neasden, before becoming a Mancunian, first at Gorton in November 1962. Its final home was at Bolton, where it arrived from Trafford Park in November 1964. Diagrammed for a duty to which it was well-suited, No 42249 calls at Lostock Junction with the 12.10pm SO Wigan Wallgate-Rochdale all-stations service on 6 November 1965. The station closed on 7 November 1966, although a new station on the site was opened in 1988, but with platforms only on the Preston lines, seen on the left of the photograph. *Brian Magilton*

With its Miles Platting, Manchester, factory becoming cramped during the 1880s, and with little room for much needed expansion, the L&YR looked to relocate its locomotive works. The company finally settled on a greenfield site at Horwich, near Bolton, in the shadow of the West Pennine Moors.

The first engine constructed was 2-4-2T No 1008 (now preserved at the National Railway Museum, York) and prior to the 1923 Grouping a total of 1,353 steam locomotives were built, including five 18in gauge engines for internal works duties. Under LMS auspices 315 locomotives were assembled and after Nationalisation in 1948 a further 172. The last locomotive to be built at Horwich was BR Standard Class 4 2-6-0 No 76099 in 1957. Amongst other types manufactured in later years were Hughes/Fowler 'Crab' 2-6-0s, Stanier 'Black 5' 4-6-0s and '8F' 2-8-0s, together with two batches of the Ivatt Class 4 Moguls.

Receiving attention inside the erecting shop on 15 June 1963, and seemingly from the far-flung corners of BR, are Southern Region BR Standard Class 4 No 76030 from Brighton (75A) and Scottish-based Ivatt 2-6-0 No 43133 of Hurlford (67B) — the latter had been built at Horwich in 1951. A couple of Stanier '8Fs' are also in view while the smokebox door of North Eastern Region Standard No 76045 from West Auckland (51F) lies propped on the floor. That day, scattered around the works were 45 steam locomotives and nine diesel shunters; the former included six permanently allocated to Horwich for duties around the site and nine awaiting cutting-up — having been withdrawn during the previous six months.

Sadly, the following year '8F' No 48756 became the last steam locomotive outshopped from Horwich, departing with due ceremony on 6 May 1964. *Dave Hampson*

Left:
Examples of two ex-L&YR classes await their fate at the back of Horwich Works on 5 April 1959 shortly after withdrawal. Nos 51404 and 51397 were originally Barton Wright Class 23 0-6-0s built by Vulcan Foundry in 1883 and 1880 respectively. Both were rebuilt as 0-6-0STs in 1895 under Aspinall's direction. For many years five of the class were retained to shunt the works, keeping their LMS numbers in the 113xx series. Furthest away is Aspinall Class 5 '2P' 2-4-2T No 50647, constructed at Horwich in 1890, a type very familiar on local passenger turns on the former L&YR system. *R. E. Gee*

Below left:
Simmering at Horwich on 16 September 1965 auto-fitted BR Standard Class 2 2-6-2T No 84025 awaits the signal to move the two non-corridor coaches into the platform road to form the 4.57pm service to Chorley. The scene is typical of many small branch line termini of the period; note the small goods shed on the left — the loading gauge outside — and the neat station buildings.

During its last years, trains on the 1870-opened branch from Blackrod on the Manchester-Preston line, known locally as the 'Horwich Jerk', had been timetabled at peak times only and mainly for the convenience of staff employed at Horwich Works who enjoyed concessionary travel terms. Thus, in the climate of the 1960s, it came as no surprise when closure proposals were announced, the last passenger departure from Horwich being the 12.5pm SO to Bolton on 25 September 1965. The train left behind Stanier 2-6-4T No 42626 which was suitably adorned with an appropriate headboard and wreath. Goods facilities continued to be provided until the following April and thereafter the branch remained open to serve the former locomotive works site only. *Barrie Walker*

Stanier Class 5 4-6-0 No 45156 *Ayrshire Yeomanry* climbs steadily along the 1 in 74 incline over the nine-arch Entwistle Viaduct, above Wayoh Reservoir, amidst the West Pennine Moors, on the demanding ex-L&YR route from Bolton to Blackburn, with the GC Enterprises tour from Stockport to Carnforth on Sunday 4 August 1968. In steam days banking of freight trains was a regular feature over the seven miles from Bolton to Waltons Sidings — just short of the 2,015yd-long Sough Tunnel.

This was a somewhat epic day in Lancashire with no fewer than six enthusiasts' specials plying the County Palatine to mark the end of regular steam on BR. Monday would dawn cold, drab and steamless, and all that remained to whet the appetite of the steam connoisseur would be the final 15 guinea commemorative special the following Sunday, which also passed Entwistle *en route* from Liverpool to Carlisle via Manchester and return.

No 45156 was one of only five 'Black 5s', all originally based in Scotland, to be personalised by a name in normal service, although No (4)5155 only carried its *Queens Edinburgh* plates from 1942 to 1944. *Ayrshire Yeomanry* came south from St Rollox (65B), along with No 45154 *Lanarkshire Yeomanry*, to Newton Heath in April 1957. No 45156 was not parted from its sister until December 1962 when the former moved to Bolton for five months before being relocated to Warrington (Dallam) (8B) for one month. No 45156 then passed to Edge Hill (8A) before returning to Manchester, this time to Patricroft, in May 1968 and thence to Rose Grove (10F) when the former closed on 1 July 1968. The locomotive was withdrawn after this excursion. *Derek Huntriss*

Below:

The grim reality that the end of steam is nigh is epitomised by this photograph at Patricroft shed shortly before its closure on 1 July 1968. It depicts withdrawn Caprotti valve gear-fitted BR Standard Class 5 4-6-0 No 73143, its connecting rod dismantled and tied to the running plate, ready for its final journey to the breakers' yard.

Built at Derby in 1956, No 73143 was one of 359 standard gauge steam locomotives in capital stock at the start of 1968, 161 being maintained between six Manchester area sheds. The shutters were brought down at Trafford Park on 4 March 1968, followed by Heaton Mersey and Stockport (Edgeley) two months later, while Bolton and Newton Heath, together with Patricroft succumbed from 1 July, just five weeks before the death knell of BR steam on normal services.

Little doubt, since its Liverpool & Manchester Railway forebears first steamed into Manchester Liverpool Road station in 1830, the iron horse had served the area with distinction, its outstanding contribution to the social and economic fabric of the region unquantifiable. It would be remembered with deep affection by many who were privileged to know it in its heyday, both those who lived among it and those who came to witness its last gasp in 1968. The steam locomotive had indeed been an outstanding and loyal servant for nearly 140 years — from the pioneering days of the Stephensons until the designs of Stanier and Riddles held sway. Its memory unquestionably deserves never to fade. *Frank Cronin*

Back cover:

In 1929, for both operational and passenger convenience, the LMS extended platform 11 at Manchester Victoria to join platform 3 at Exchange, creating, at 2,235ft, the longest station platform in Britain. On 24 September 1966 the photographer utilises platform 3 at Exchange to silhouette BR Standard Class 5 4-6-0 No 73045 as it emerges into daylight, while returning light engine to Patricroft shed from Red Bank sidings, having passed through earlier with some empty newspaper vans.

Trains travelling between Salford and Manchester Victoria passed outside the station wall on the right, while conversely passengers boarding Yorkshire-bound services at Exchange passed through the middle of Victoria station at the start of their journey east. On the left can be seen the tower of Sacred Trinity church, the nave being at street level below, while another familiar landmark to Manchester enginemen, as were its affiliated establishments, Threlfall's Brewery, can be seen behind No 73045. Manchester Exchange closed on 5 May 1969. *Brian Magilton*